MONSTER HIGH

I Only Have EYL... You

An **ORIGINAL**
Graphic Novel

Written by
Heather Nuhfer

Illustrated by
Kellee Riley

L B

LITTLE, BROWN AND COMPANY
NEW YORK BOSTON

This book is a work of fiction. Names, characters, places, and incidents are the product of the author's imagination or are used fictitiously. Any resemblance to actual events, locales, or persons, living or dead, is coincidental.

Copyright © 2014 Mattel, Inc. All rights reserved. MONSTER HIGH and associated trademarks are owned by and used under license from Mattel, Inc.

Special thanks to Venetia Davie, Tanya Mann, Darren Sander, Julia Phelps, Garrett Sander, Charnita Belcher, Sharon Woloszyk, and Andrea Isasi.
Cover art by Kellee Riley
Cover design by Christina Quintero
Interior inks and colors by Kellee Riley
Bubbles and lettering by Kellee Riley and Ching Nga Chan

In accordance with the U.S. Copyright Act of 1976, the scanning, uploading, and electronic sharing of any part of this book without the permission of the publisher is unlawful piracy and theft of the author's intellectual property. If you would like to use material from the book (other than for review purposes), prior written permission must be obtained by contacting the publisher at permissions@hbgusa.com. Thank you for your support of the author's rights.

Little, Brown and Company

Hachette Book Group
1290 Avenue of the Americas, New York, NY 10104
Visit us at lb-kids.com
monsterhigh.com

Little, Brown and Company is a division of Hachette Book Group, Inc.
The Little, Brown name and logo are trademarks of Hachette Book Group, Inc.

The publisher is not responsible for websites (or their content) that are not owned by the publisher.

First Edition: December 2014

Library of Congress Control Number: 2014943618

ISBN 978-0-316-28286-4

10 9 8 7 6 5 4 3 2 1

CW

Printed in the United States of America

TABLE OF CONTENTS

WHO'S WHO

FRANKIE STEIN

MONSTER PARENTS: FRANKENSTEIN AND HIS BRIDE
AGE: HOW MANY DAYS HAS IT BEEN?
FRANKIE IS SPARKING WITH ENTHUSIASM FOR UNLIFE AT MONSTER HIGH. SHE MAY SOMETIMES FALL APART AT THE SEAMS, BUT SHE IS ALWAYS THERE TO LEND A HELPING HAND.

CLAWDEEN WOLF

MONSTER PARENTS: THE WEREWOLVES
AGE: 15
CLAWDEEN IS BOLD, OPINIONATED, AND FIERCELY LOYAL TO HER FRIENDS. SHE IS THE YOUNGER SISTER OF CLAWDIA AND CLAWD, AND SHE IS HOWLEEN'S OLDER SISTER.

CLEO DE NILE

MONSTER PARENT: THE MUMMY
AGE: 5,842 (GIVE OR TAKE A FEW YEARS)
AN ACTUAL EGYPTIAN PRINCESS, CLEO RULES THE HALLS OF MONSTER HIGH AS CAPTAIN OF THE FEAR SQUAD. WHILE A BIT SELF-CENTERED, CLEO IS A TRUE FRIEND.

DRACULAURA

MONSTER PARENT: DRACULA
AGE: 1,600
DRACULAURA IS KIND, GENEROUS, AND SCARY-SWEET. SHE IS A VEGETARIAN VAMPIRE AND A HOPELESS ROMANTIC.

GHOULIA YELPS

MONSTER PARENTS: ZOMBIES
AGE: 16
GHOULIA MAY MOVE A BIT SLOWLY, BUT SHE'S THE SMARTEST GHOUL AT MONSTER HIGH. SHE SPEAKS ONLY IN ZOMBESE, WHICH MOST MONSTERS CAN EASILY UNDERSTAND.

ABBEY BOMINABLE

MONSTER PARENT: THE YETI
AGE: 16
ABBEY IS ENORMOUSLY STRONG AND AS BLUNT AS A HAMMER. HER WORDS CAN COME ACROSS AS COLD AND HARSH, BUT SHE HAS A WARM HEART.

HEATH BURNS

MONSTER PARENTS: FIRE ELEMENTALS
AGE: 15
HEATH HAS A GOOD HEART, BUT HE TENDS TO CAUSE A LITTLE CHAOS WHEN THINGS HEAT UP!

IRIS CLOPS

MONSTER PARENT: THE CYCLOPS

AGE: 15

IRIS IS A LITTLE BIT SHY AND A LITTLE BIT CLUMSY—PROBABLY DUE TO HER LACK OF DEPTH PERCEPTION! BUT SHE HAS A KEEN EYE FOR FASHION.

MANNY TAUR

MONSTER PARENT: THE MINOTAUR

AGE: 16

MANNY IS LARGER THAN YOUR AVERAGE MONSTER AND TENDS TO KNOCK THINGS OVER, WHICH EMBARRASSES HIM. BUT HE'S UP FOR ANY COMPETITION, WHETHER IT'S FOOTBALL, CASKETBALL, OR SKRM!

GILLINGTON "GIL" WEBBER

MONSTER PARENT: THE RIVER MONSTER

AGE: 16

GIL CAN'T HELP LOVING HIS SEA MONSTER GAL, LAGOONA. DESPITE HIS FEAR OF THE OCEAN, HIS HELMET KEEPS HIS HEAD HYDRATED WHEN HE'S NOT SWIMMING.

LAGOONA BLUE

MONSTER PARENT: THE SEA MONSTER

AGE: 15

LAGOONA'S LAID-BACK STYLE PLAYS WELL WITH HER LOVE OF SPORTS. SHE'D LOVE TO BE SWIMMING ALL THE TIME!

SCARAH SCREAMS

 MONSTER PARENT: THE BEAN SÍ (BANSHEE)

AGE: 15

SCARAH CAN READ OTHER PEOPLE'S MINDS, BUT SHE TRIES TO BE POLITE ABOUT IT.

INVISI BILLY

 MONSTER PARENT: THE INVISIBLE MAN

AGE: 15

BILLY CAN HIDE IN PLAIN SIGHT IF HE WANTS TO, WHICH COMES IN HANDY WHEN HE'S WORKING BACKSTAGE FOR MONSTER HIGH THEATER PRODUCTIONS!

CLAWD WOLF

MONSTER PARENTS: THE WEREWOLVES

AGE: 17

CLAWD IS THE QUARTERBACK OF THE FOOTBALL TEAM AND THE CAPTAIN OF THE CASKETBALL TEAM. BUT HE'S NO DUMB JOCK. HE IS THE OLDER BROTHER OF CLAWDEEN AND HOWLEEN, AND HE'S DATING DRACULAURA.

DEUCE GORGON

 MONSTER PARENT: MEDUSA

AGE: 16

THIS CHILL CASKETBALL PLAYER LOVES TO COOK AND IS ONE-HALF OF THE POWER COUPLE ON CAMPUS WITH CLEO DE NILE.

IRIS and MANNY

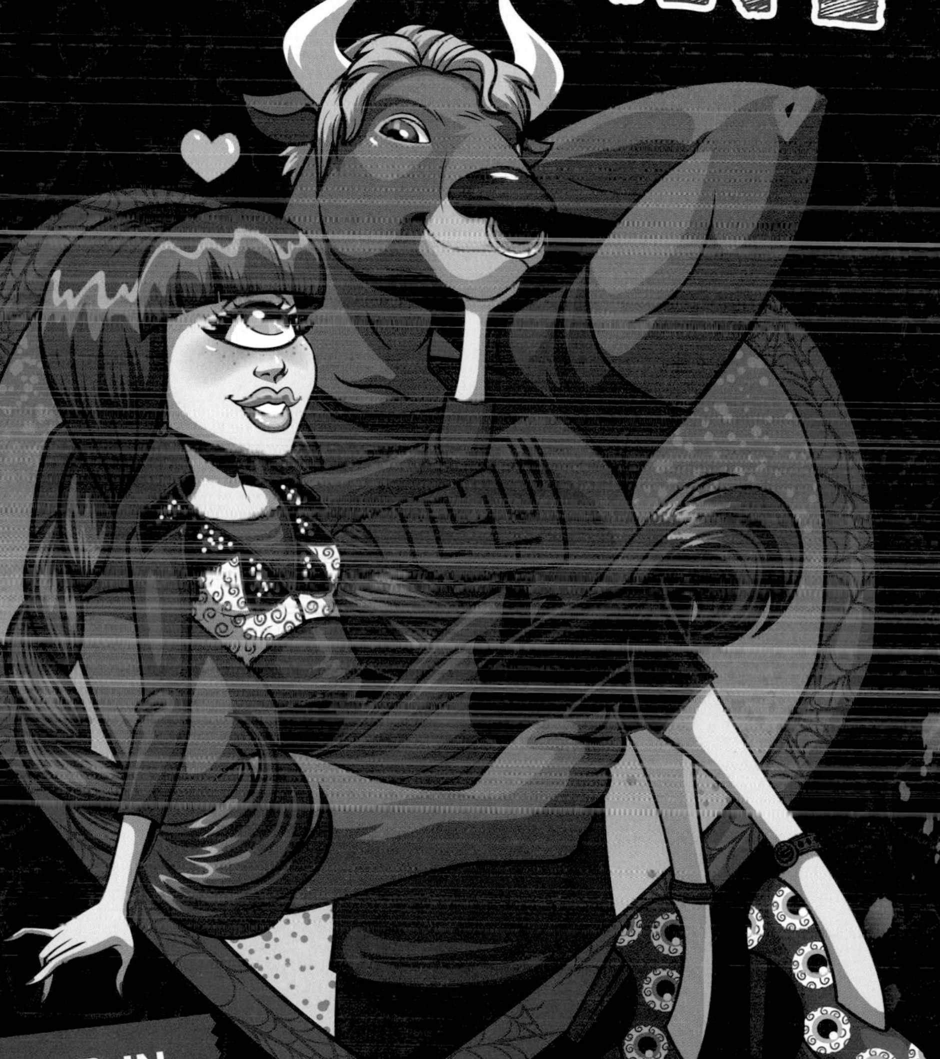

STAR IN

BULL'S EYE

LAGOONA and GIL

STAR IN

LOCKETNESS MONSTER

HOW FINTASTIC! I'M SUCH A LUCKY GHOUL!

GIL, WOULD YOU BE MY DATE FOR THE FRAIDY HAWKINS DANCE?

OF COURSE!

RIIIIING!!

OH, CRIKEY! I NEED TO GO! I TOLD VENUS I'D HELP HER PICK UP TRASH IN THE QUAD DURING MY FREE PERIOD!

BYE, GIL! SEE YOU LATER!

LAGOONA! YOU FORGOT YOUR...

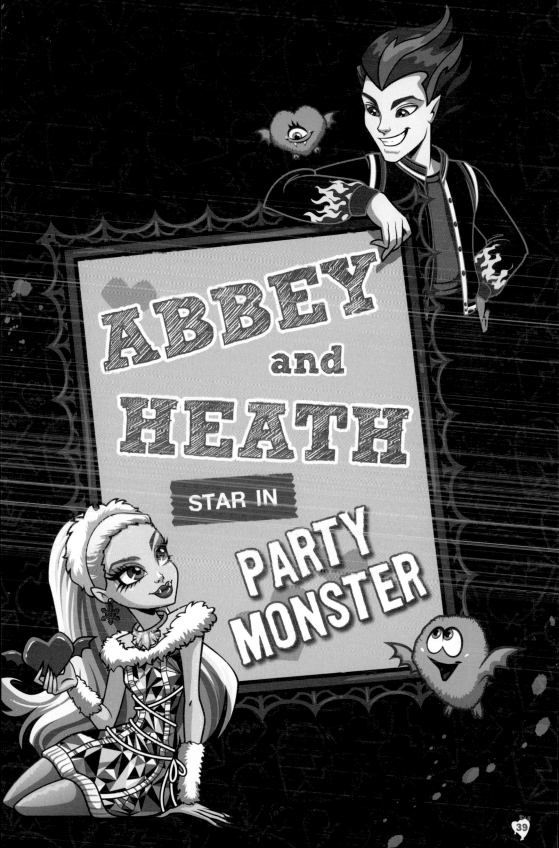

ABBEY
and
HEATH
STAR IN
PARTY
MONSTER

HEY, ABBEY!

HELLO, HEATH. EXCUSE, I AM VERY BUSY.

WHATCHA DOIN?

HAVE **BIG** ORDER OF FURRY FIENDS TODAY! DOING VERY WELL. MUST HURRY TO DELIVER THEM. MUST NOT BE LATE.

OH! I THOUGHT YOU FOUND A BIG PILE OF HAIRBALLS OR SOMETHING!

SIT!

YET! SHAKES IN BOOTS WHEN I COME AROUND! NO FLUFFY BALL SCARE ME.

THUD!

YOU LOOK... FAMILIAR.

COUSIN OF SHIVER, PERHAPS?

NO...

GASP!

HEATH?

WHAT HAVE YOU DONE? WE MUST FIND GHOULIA.

THANKS FOR YOUR HELP, GHOULIA. BOYS, EH?

<THERE'S ALWAYS ONE WHO WANTS TO PLAY MAD SCIENTIST.>

BZZZT!

*TRANSLATED FROM ZOMBESE

GEEZ, I'M REALLY SORRY, GHOULIA! I PROMISE I WON'T MESS WITH YOUR LAB STUFF EVER AGAIN!

<I SHOULD REALLY GET AN ASP SECURITY SYSTEM FROM CLEO.>*

UMM...YEP.

UH, YEAH...A POISONOUS SNAKE **WOULD** PROBABLY MAKE A GREAT SECURITY GUARD!

THANK YOU, GHOULIA.

SCARAH and INVISI BILLY

STAR IN

SHOCK AND AWW!

PURRR...

SUCH A MASSIVE DOSE OF THE CUTE—I CAN BARELY STAND IT!

WHY DIDN'T MINE WORK?

OH, SOMETIMES IT TAKES TWO JOLTS! LET ME CHARGE UP FOR A MINUTE.

INVISI BILLY, SO THE FRAIDY HAWKINS DANCE IS SOON....I WAS WONDERING IF MAYBE YOU WOULD WANT TO...

YES?

CLEO and DEUCE

STAR IN

TABLE FOR NONE

OH, WOW! AREN'T THEY VOLTAGEOUS?

<THEY WOULD BE PERFECT FOR FRAIDY HAWKINS!>*

YOU'RE RIGHT, GHOULIA!

*TRANSLATED FROM ZOMBESE

70

...BUT I HAVE NEVER APPROVED OF THIS BOY AND CERTAINLY WILL NOT FUND YOUR DATE WITH HIM!

THAT BOY IS AS LOW ON THE PYRAMID AS YOU CAN GET. I WILL NEVER APPROVE!

I KNOW YOU DON'T LIKE HIM, DADDY, BUT DEUCE IS MY BOYFRIEND, AND HE'S ALWAYS BEEN THERE FOR ME. HE'S A ROYALLY GOOD MANSTER!

GO TO YOUR ROOM! I WILL NOT GIVE YOU MORE MONEY TO SPEND ON A DATE WITH THAT SNAKEY-HAIRED BOY!

FINE THEN! I'M SURE DEUCE HAS BEEN SAVING UP TO GIVE ME EVERY LITTLE THING MY HEART DESIRES!

AND TELL THAT BOY HE NEEDS TO WORK ON HIS PHONE MANNERS!

"PHONE MANNERS"? I THINK YOU'VE BEEN SPENDING TOO MUCH TIME IN YOUR SARCOPHAGUS, DAD. TIME TO GET SOME FRESH AIR.

DRACULAURA and CLAWD

STAR IN

SHADOW OF A DOUBT

"...AS LONG AS HE'S AT THE DANCE WITH ME, EVERYTHING WILL BE CREEPTASTIC!"

CLAWD SHOULD BE HERE SOON.

IF NOT, WE LEAVE HIM OUT IN THE COLD. FOREVER.

HE'LL BE HERE ANY SECOND. I KNOW IT!

HERE HE IS!

SO WE'RE JUST SUPPOSED TO BELIEVE YOU? AFTER YOU PUT A SPELL ON DRACULAURA AND TRIED TO STEAL HER HEART AT HER OWN SWEET 1600 BIRTHDAY PARTY*?

LITERALLY!

YOU SHOULD HAVE LEARNED THEN, VALENTINE, THAT MY HEART BELONGS TO ONE MONSTER—

IT'S TRUE! I'VE BEEN HELPING ALL OF YOU FOR WEEKS!

I EVEN DID IT IN SECRET TO SHOW YOU I'M TURNING OVER A NEW TOMBSTONE!

*SEE THE BOO-VIE WHY DO GHOULS FALL IN LOVE? FOR THE FULL STORY.

PERSONALLY, I'D CHOSE "PROVE IT," DUDE.

HAS NO ONE NOTICED?

PROVE IT—OR FEEL MY WRATH.

MANNY! IRIS! AT THE MOVIES I TOOK ALL OF IRIS'S CANDY SO MANNY WOULD HAVE TO BE VALIANT AND GET HER MORE.

I TOTALLY EMBARRASSED MYSELF BECAUSE OF YOU!

STUPID STICKY HOOVES...

AND I MADE SURE GIL FOUND THE BIGGEST SEASHELL EVER TO IMPRESS LAGOONA! DO YOU KNOW HOW HARD IT IS TO GET A SHELL FROM A SCARY SEA WITCH?!

IT WAS AN ENCHANTED SHELL, THOUGH.

CAUSED A BIT OF TROUBLE, MATE.

ACTUALLY, IF YOU REALLY LOOK HARD AT IT, VALENTINE HELPED US ALL!

OR HAD SO MUCH FUN TOGETHER.

IF MANNY HADN'T GOTTEN COVERED IN STICKY CANDY, I NEVER WOULD HAVE FOUND OUT WHY HE WAS SO UPSET AND ASKED HIM TO THE DANCE!

OR MADE SOME ANIMAL FRIENDS.

OR SHARED A SECRET.

OR KISSED EVERYONE!

TURNS OUT YOU REALLY DID HELP EVERYONE!

I DID?... I DID!

HEATHER NUHFER

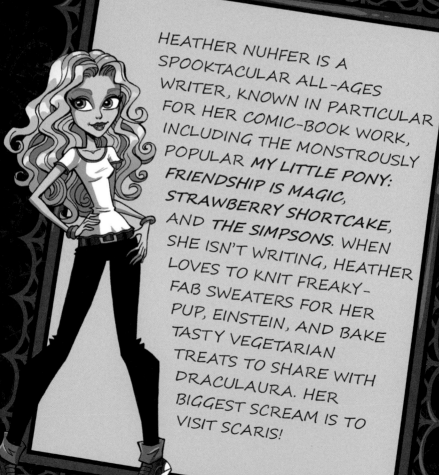

HEATHER NUHFER IS A SPOOKTACULAR ALL-AGES WRITER, KNOWN IN PARTICULAR FOR HER COMIC-BOOK WORK, INCLUDING THE MONSTROUSLY POPULAR *MY LITTLE PONY: FRIENDSHIP IS MAGIC*, *STRAWBERRY SHORTCAKE*, AND *THE SIMPSONS*. WHEN SHE ISN'T WRITING, HEATHER LOVES TO KNIT FREAKY-FAB SWEATERS FOR HER PUP, EINSTEIN, AND BAKE TASTY VEGETARIAN TREATS TO SHARE WITH DRACULAURA. HER BIGGEST SCREAM IS TO VISIT SCARIS!

KELLEE RILEY

KELLEE RILEY IS A FRIGHTENINGLY BUSY ILLUSTRATOR WHO HAS WORKED ON OVER TWENTY MAJOR BRANDS, INCLUDING BARBIE, MY LITTLE PONY, DORA THE EXPLORER, AND MANY MORE. MOST NOTED AS THE ORIGINAL ILLUSTRATOR ON MONSTER HIGH, SHE ALSO HAS OVER FORTY CHILDREN'S BOOKS TO HER CREDIT. KELLEE LOVES COMICS, VIDEO GAMES, AND DRESSING UP IN FUN OUTFITS TO MATCH HER FANGTASTIC WIG COLLECTION.

AVAILABLE NOW!

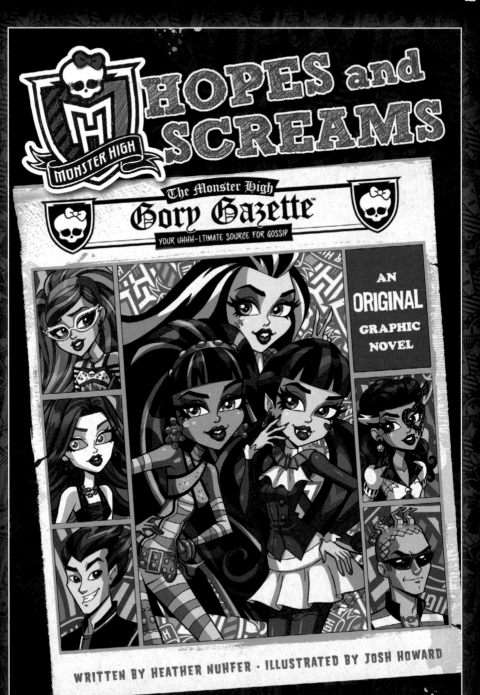

WRITTEN BY HEATHER NUHFER · ILLUSTRATED BY JOSH HOWARD

Read howl about
Frankie Stein and the
Gory Gazette in the first
Monster High graphic novel!
Turn the page for a peek at
Cleo de Nile's story from
Hopes and Screams!

*TRANSLATED FROM ZOMBESE

READ THE GHOULFRIENDS SERIES
BY GITTY DANESHVARI!